Collecting Small Fossils

COLLECTING

SMALL FOSSILS

By Lois J. Hussey and
Catherine Pessino

Illustrated by Anne Marie Jauss

THOMAS Y. CROWELL COMPANY   NEW YORK

Designed by Mina Baylis

Manufactured in the United States of America

L. C. Card 77–101932

ISBN 0–690–19733–0
0–690–19734–9 (Lib. Ed.)

1   2   3   4   5   6   7   8   9   10

BY THE AUTHORS

Collecting Cocoons

Collecting Small Fossils

What Is a Fossil?

Fossils are clues to life in the past. They are the remains or other evidences of animals and plants that lived a long time ago, at least ten thousand years ago.

The fossils described in this book are the ones you are most likely to find. They are easy to recognize and to collect. They can be found over most of the United States and in Canada.

These are the fossils of invertebrates. Invertebrates are animals without backbones. In fact, invertebrates have no bones at all. Some common invertebrates are clams, jellyfish, worms, and insects.

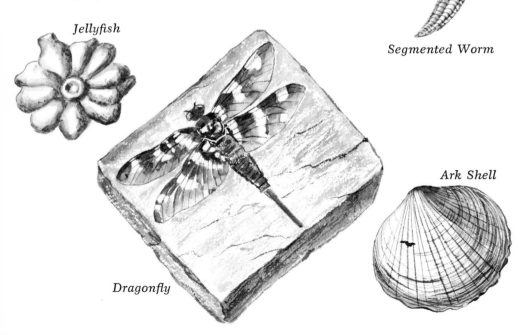

Jellyfish

Segmented Worm

Ark Shell

Dragonfly

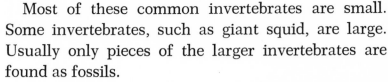

Most of these common invertebrates are small. Some invertebrates, such as giant squid, are large. Usually only pieces of the larger invertebrates are found as fossils.

Most of the invertebrate fossils that you find will be the shells or other hard parts of the animals. The soft parts will have rotted away.

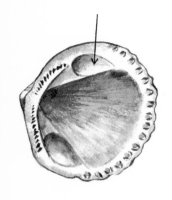

That is what happened to this fossil shell. Only the hard part is left. The arrow shows where a large muscle once was attached.

Quite often the fossil remains that you find will be petrified (stony). As this shell lay buried in the ground, water, containing minerals, covered the shell. The water filled tiny spaces in the shell, spaces too small to see without a magnifying glass. When the water evaporated, the minerals were left in the shell, making it stony.

In some petrified fossils all of the shell or other remains have been replaced over a long period of time by minerals.

Many fossils that you find will not be the remains of animals, but impressions of their shells or other hard parts which have since disappeared. Here we see the fossil impression of the outside of a shell. This is an external (outer) mold.

Here is the fossil impression of the inside of a shell. This is an internal (inner) mold.

This natural fossil cast was formed when the mold became filled with sand which then hardened into stone.

Rarely is a fossil hunter lucky enough to find the remains of the soft parts of an animal, or even an impression of a soft part. Rarer still is a fossil of an animal without any hard parts at all, such as this fossil impression of a jellyfish.

Some fossil impressions are thin, shiny, black impressions. The black is carbon, the only substance left after the animal rotted away. This is a carbon impression of an insect.

Some of the small fossils that you will find are neither the remains of animals nor the impressions of animals, but their tracks and traces, such as

this fossil trail left by a snail

these burrows made by a worm

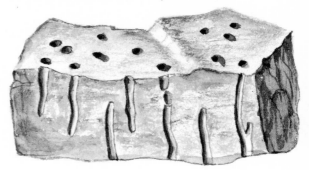

the hole made by a snail that attacked
this clam

the borings made by a sponge that
lived on this shell

this casting from a worm

Until now only animals have been mentioned. But plants, too, are found as fossils. In fact, in some areas, plant fossils are more common than those of animals. Some of the common plant fossils are also included in this book.

The study of fossils is called paleontology. The scientist who studies fossils is called a paleontologist.

How Fossils Are Formed

Only a few of the many animals and plants that once lived have been preserved as fossils. Most animals and plants are eaten, or decay and disappear. Those that are buried by mud, sand, or volcanic ash soon after dying are the ones most likely to be preserved. These layers of mud, sand, or volcanic ash are called sediments.

Because animals that live in the sea have the best chance of being buried by soft sediments soon after dying, marine invertebrates (invertebrates of the sea) are among the most common fossils.

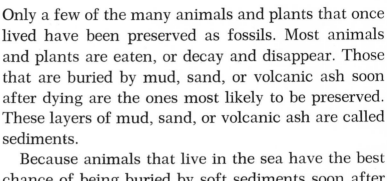

A snail living in the sea dies.
It falls to the bottom.
It settles down into the soft sand or mud.
The soft parts decay. Only the hard
    shell is left.

In time the shell is buried under many
   layers of sand or mud.
The weight of the layers on top press
   down on the lower layers.
This causes the lower layers to be
   cemented together, forming layers
   of rock.

Later the sea dries up.
The land erodes away, exposing the
   layers of rock.
Continued erosion exposes the fossil.
It can now be found.
320 million years passed from the time
   this snail died until it was found
   as a fossil.

Pseudofossils

Pseudo means "false." Pseudofossils are not fossils; they only look like fossils. In hunting for fossils you may also find pseudofossils. A few common ones are shown below.

CONCRETIONS.   Some rocks have unusual shapes which resemble plants or animals.

DENDRITES.   Some minerals leave plantlike deposits on rocks.

Obsidian.   Some minerals break in
such a way that they appear to be
the mold of a shell.

Some rocks weather in such a way
that they assume shapes which
appear to be teeth, footprints, or
other evidences of animals or
plants.

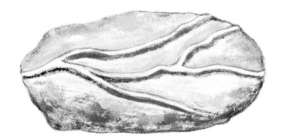

Sedimentary Rocks

Rock formed from sediments is called sedimentary rock. There are different types of sedimentary rock. For example:

Rock made from sediments of sand is called sandstone.

Rock made from sediments of mud and clay is called shale.

Rock made from plant remains is called coal.

Rock made from sediments of lime is called limestone.

Rock made from sediments of volcanic ash is called tuff.

Shale, sandstone, and limestone are the most common sedimentary rocks.

It is in sedimentary rock that we look for fossils. Fossils are rarely found in other kinds of rock.

Fortunately for the fossil hunter, more than 80 percent of this country is covered with sedimentary rock. The flat lands and hills and even the mountains about you are probably made of sedimentary rock.

Not *all* sedimentary rock contains fossils. It may be that no plants or animals lived at the time and place when the rock was being formed; or, perhaps, conditions were not right for plants and animals to become fossils. In some sedimentary rock, fossils, though present, may be buried too deeply within the layers of rock to be found.

Distribution of Sedimentary Rock

How Old Is It?

Geologists, scientists who study rocks, are able to tell by laboratory tests how old a rock is—that is, how long ago the rock was formed. Fossils are the same age as the rock in which they are found.

Certain animals lived only during a certain period. Fossils of these animals are found only in rocks of that same period. When these same fossils are found in rocks that have not yet been dated by geologists, the fossils indicate the age of the rocks. These fossils are called index fossils.

It takes thousands and thousands of years for rocks to be formed. The oldest rocks are thought to be at least 4½ billion years old.

To make it easier to talk about such a vast length of time, geologists have divided the past into periods. Most of these periods are named for the places where rocks of that particular age were first studied by geologists. For example, the Pennsylvanian period is named after the coal regions of Pennsylvania.

Because it will help you to tell the age of the fossils you find, and help you with other references, you will want to be familiar with the names of the periods. The oldest period is at the bottom of the list, for that is the way the rock layers were formed, with the oldest at the bottom, and the youngest at the top.

Period	*Time*
QUATERNARY	Present to 1.5 million years ago
TERTIARY	1.5 million to 65 million years ago
CRETACEOUS	65 million to 135 million years ago
JURASSIC	135 million to 192 million years ago
TRIASSIC	192 million to 225 million years ago
PERMIAN	225 million to 280 million years ago
PENNSYLVANIAN	280 million to 320 million years ago
MISSISSIPPIAN	320 million to 345 million years ago
DEVONIAN	345 million to 395 million years ago
SILURIAN	395 million to 435 million years ago
ORDOVICIAN	435 million to 500 million years ago
CAMBRIAN	500 million to 570 million years ago

All time before the Cambrian is called Precambrian. The Precambrian era ended with the start of the Cambrian period, 570 million years ago. A few fossils have been found from the Precambrian era, but most fossils that are found date from after the start of the Cambrian period.

In older references you may find different dates from the ones given here. As more work is done on dating rocks, the dates are changed.

Fossils Are Clues to Prehistoric Times

The land looked very different in past periods from what it does today. This is known from the fossils that are found. They are clues to past life.

For example, these fossils are all from the Pennsylvanian period. From these and other fossils of the

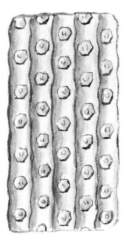

Giant Club Moss (Sigillaria) section of bark showing leaf scars

Giant Horsetail

Seed Fern

Scouring Rush

same period, paleontologists know that the land in
many parts of the United States 280 million to 320
million years ago looked like this:

PENNSYLVANIAN FOREST

Giant Club Mosses
(Sigillaria)

Giant Club Moss
(Lepidodendron)

Tree Fern

An early Conifer

Giant Horsetails

Club Moss trunk and a Seed Fern

Life in the seas, too, was different in past periods.

DEVONIAN SEA

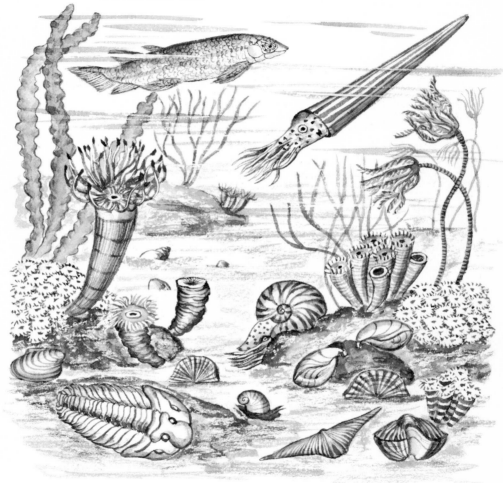

Lungfish   Straight-shelled Nautiloid   Sea Lilies

Bivalve Corals   Ammonoid Snail   Rugose and Colonial Corals

Trilobite   Brachiopods

Where to Start
Looking for Fossils

No matter where you live, whether in a city or in the country, the search for fossils is the same. First, let people know that you are interested in fossils and that you want to collect them. Ask your parents and teachers if they know where fossils might be found. Any geologists, paleontologists, or amateur rock collectors living in your neighborhood will know where to look for fossils. Is there a local geology club where you can inquire? Is there a rock or mineral dealer who might be able to help?

People who work out of doors, such as construction workers, highway engineers, farmers, ranchers, and well diggers, often come across fossils in their work. They may know of some good areas to search for fossils.

BOOKS

Look in your school or public library for books about fossils.

COLLECTIONS

Find out whether a local museum, college, or university has a collection of fossils on display. Visit the collection and read the labels to see where the fossils were found. Perhaps some were found in your area. The curator, the person in charge of the collection, may be able to help you. Get in touch with him by mail or by telephone.

GEOLOGICAL SURVEYS

Each state (and Canadian province) has a government division called the geological survey. Some have published fossil guides. Write to your state geological survey and ask for a fossil guide to your state. If none is available, ask their help in finding a site where you could collect small fossils. Frequently, the geological survey will refer you to maps.

MAPS

Maps are useful guides for the fossil hunter. The paleontologist uses three kinds of maps:

A *road map* is the one most people use. It shows roads and rivers, lakes and bridges. It shows the location of towns and cities. Once you learn the name of a good collecting spot, you can locate it on a road map.

The map will help you decide how best to get there. Road maps are given away at gas stations.

A *topographic map* shows all the things found on a road map. It also shows the ups (hills, cliffs, mountains) and downs (valleys, river beds) of the area. It shows houses and other buildings. And it shows quarries, mine dumps, tunnels, and where highways have been cut through rock. These are places where fossil hunts often begin.

The detailed legend on the back of a topographic map will help you in reading the map. Careful study of the map will give you a good idea of how the area looks before seeing it.

A *geologic map* shows all the things found on a road map and on a topographic map. It also indicates the type of bedrock in the area. Bedrock is the solid and continuous rock of the earth's crust.

Because fossils are usually found in sedimentary rock, look at a geologic map to see where the bedrock is sedimentary.

The bedrock is not always visible. It is often buried beneath the surface. That is why the fossil hunter looks for building excavations, highway cuts, quarries, mine dumps, and tunnels, places where bedrock is exposed.

Topographic maps and geologic maps may be purchased from the United States Geological Survey.

Collecting Equipment

A pair of sharp eyes, patience, and luck are needed when fossil hunting. Little equipment is needed. You may already have most of the equipment.

HAMMER (*geologist's, mason's, or bricklayer's*). An ordinary hammer is not suitable for breaking rock. You will need to get a geologist's hammer or one used by stone masons or bricklayers. The square head on these hammers is designed for breaking off rock. The other end, which is either a pointed pick or a chisel, is used for digging, prying, and for splitting soft rock. A mason's or bricklayer's hammer may be purchased at a hardware store. A geologist's hammer may be purchased from a rock dealer or from a biological supply house.

STEEL CHISELS.   Steel chisels of various sizes are used in prying specimens from rock. A ½-inch chisel and a 1-inch chisel are the most useful sizes for the beginner.

AWL AND CORK.   A small pointed awl is useful in prying small specimens from soft rock. When the awl isn't in use the pointed end is kept buried in a cork.

SAFETY GOGGLES.   Always wear safety goggles when breaking hard rock to protect your eyes from flying chips. Safety goggles may be purchased at hardware stores.

WORK GLOVES.   Heavy work gloves will protect your hands should the chisel or hammer slip. The gloves will also protect you from sliver-like rock fragments.

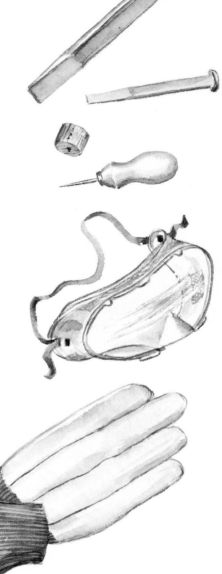

23

WHISKBROOM. This is useful to clear away loose soil, rock, and other debris.

NEWSPAPER. The fossils you collect should be wrapped in newspaper to protect them.

SMALL BOXES AND COTTON OR TISSUES. Very small or very fragile specimens may be protected with cotton or tissues and placed in small boxes.

KNAPSACK OR OTHER BAG. Any strong, lightweight, inexpensive bag can be used as a collecting bag. Knapsacks, flour sacks, or old school bags are suitable. A bag with a shoulder strap is convenient.

NOTEBOOK, BALLPOINT PEN, ADHESIVE OR MASKING TAPE. These are needed for recording information.

MAGNIFYING GLASS.   A magnifying
  glass is useful but not necessary. If
  you plan to buy one, get a 10 power
  ($10 \times$) hand lens. It may be purchased at a store selling optical
  equipment.

GUIDE BOOK AND MAPS.   If you have a
  small fossil guide for the area in
  which you are collecting, you may
  want to take it along.

BAND-AIDS.   Just in case.

CANTEEN, SANDWICH, CANDY BAR.   Most
  collectors get thirsty and hungry in
  the field. Be sure to carry some
  water and a snack.

The Collecting Trip

BEFORE STARTING OUT

It is best to go on your first collecting trip with an experienced fossil hunter, or with a group from a museum or local rock club. They will help you learn what to look for.

If there are no experienced fossil hunters available, and you are starting out alone or with friends to a collecting site some distance from home, it is essential that you plan your trip ahead of time.

Find the fossil site you are going to visit on a road map. Decide how best to reach it.

Is the site on private property? If so, you should get permission from the owner before starting out. Your trip may be to a commercial quarry, clay pit, or mine dump, as these are good places to start. If so, you must first write to the company and get permission to visit the place and to collect. Be prepared to obey all rules set forth by the owners. Otherwise the owners may not permit anyone to collect on their property again.

Remember that collecting is generally forbidden in

all parks, preserves, and sanctuaries. Plants, animals, and rocks, too, are protected in these areas.

Assemble all of your collecting equipment. Pack it carefully in your collecting bag. Wear sturdy shoes and work clothes.

AT THE SITE

Once you arrive at the site, you will see that the spot on the map covers a large area. Where to begin?

It is useless to look for fossils in a field covered with plants, or in a pond filled with water. Instead, look around for exposed bedrock. Remember, it must be sedimentary rock. Sedimentary rock can be recognized by its layered appearance.

Look for rock exposures at building excavations, along canyon walls, along river banks and in dry river beds, in gullies, along road cuts, in quarries, and around mines.

Look for places where sedimentary rock has been dug up, such as building excavations, well diggings, mine dumps.

Once you have found a likely spot, sit or kneel down. Pick up and examine any loose rocks. It is easier to begin with loose rock, which may contain fossils, than to break up rock.

Geologists call loose rock *float*. This means that the rock may not have come from the bedrock in the area but may have been carried there by man, or by natural forces.

Examine the bedrock. If no fossils are visible, put on your goggles and gloves and break off small pieces of bedrock with your hammer. It is easiest to break off jutting rock.

It is on the broad, flat surfaces of sedimentary rock layers that fossils will be found. Use your hammer and chisel to split open the layers of rock. Be sure to split the rock parallel to the layers. Always aim the chisel away from you.

If all this fails, move on to another likely spot and try again. Remember that patience is needed, and a certain amount of luck. Not all sedimentary rock will contain fossils. Keep looking. Do not give up.

SUCCESS

Your first fossil find is the start of your own collection. If the fossil is found lying on the ground, it need only be picked up. Before wrapping it in newspaper to carry it home, you will want to record information about the find in your notebook. This written record is an important part of a collection. The scientist calls the information data. Without accurate data a collection has no scientific value.

First, tear off a small piece of tape. Stick it on your specimen. Write the number of the specimen on the tape. If it is your first specimen, it will be No. 1.

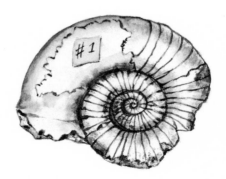

In your notebook write No. 1. Next to it record the following data: date, name of fossil if known, exact place where it was found (locate the place on your road map so that you can find the exact spot another time), the fact that the specimen was found loose, any other information that you think may be useful, and your own name as the collector.

Make it a habit to record the data as soon as you find a fossil.

When all the data has been recorded, wrap the specimen in newspaper. Use tape to hold the newspaper in place. Put the wrapped specimen in your collecting bag. If the fossil is very small or fragile, wrap it in cotton or tissues, and put it in a box before placing it in your collecting bag. Always place heavier specimens in the bottom of the bag, lighter ones on top.

To remove a fossil imbedded in bedrock, use your hammer and chisel. Use the smaller chisel for small specimens. Put on your safety goggles and gloves. Hold the chisel several inches away from the fossil so that the fossil will not be hit should the chisel slip. Aim the chisel away from you and away from the specimen. Gently tap the chisel with the hammer. Cut all around the fossil; then cut under the fossil. Once the specimen is freed from the bedrock, number it and record your data.

Do not discard broken specimens, but collect all the pieces. It may be possible to glue them together at home. Wrap each piece separately; then wrap them together in a single package. Stick the specimen number on the outside of the package.

Note: If you find any fossils that you think are rare, or specimens too large to collect easily, leave them alone and get professional help. In the past many otherwise valuable fossils have been ruined by inexperienced collectors.

When you are ready to leave, look about you. Always leave a clean site. This is only good outdoor manners.

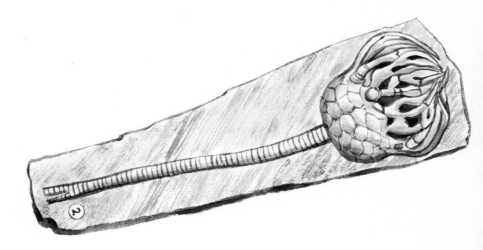

How to Clean Fossils

At home, unwrap one specimen. Select a jar, basin, or old can large enough to hold it. Put enough water in the container to cover the specimen. Remove the numbered tape. Stick it on the outside of the container. Place the specimen in the container of water. Let it soak overnight.

Next day, use an old toothbrush to remove any soil still clinging to the specimen. You can now get a better look at it, and can decide whether you need to do anything more to it.

If you want to trim excess rock from around the fossil, put on your goggles and gloves and use a small hammer and chisel. If you are working indoors, place a pile of newspapers two inches thick under the specimen to protect the floor or table. When you have finished chipping away excess rock, rinse off the specimen to remove any loose rock particles.

If the fossil is imbedded in soft rock, you can try to pry it out of the rock, using an awl, old dental tools, a nut pick, a large needle, a corsage pin, or a hat pin. A soft brush is useful to remove loose particles. Rinse off the specimen when you have finished.

The same tools are used for a final, closer cleaning of the fossil itself.

To do close work, a large magnifying glass is helpful. The glass should be mounted on a stand so that both of your hands are free to work on the specimen. If you can't devise a stand, the magnifying glass can be held by a stack of books. You may find it helpful to use a lump of clay or plasticene to hold a small specimen while working on it.

Give the specimen a final rinse. Place it on newspaper to dry alongside its identifying number.

Broken specimens can be glued together with household cement or a white glue. Hold the pieces together with rubber bands until the glue dries thoroughly; then gently clean the fossil.

A Fossil Collection

Each specimen, after it is cleaned and dried, should be permanently marked with its identification number.

First, paint a small circle with white or yellow enamel paint on the specimen. Put the circle where it will not be too noticeable. (Try doing this first on a piece of waste rock.) After the paint dries, write the specimen number on the painted circle with ink. After the ink dries, coat the painted circle with clear nail polish or shellac to prevent the number from rubbing off. With tiny fossils, place the identifying number on the box or vial that holds the fossil.

The scientist always transfers the data from his field notebook to permanent record cards. You may want to do the same. Three-by-five-inch index cards are suitable. Use one card for each specimen.

The same information you recorded in your notebook is often put on the label that is kept with a specimen, whether the specimen is on display or is stored away. Shoe boxes, cigar boxes, egg cartons, match boxes, greeting card boxes, and plastic boxes can all be used for keeping a collection.

Boxes with transparent lids are good for displaying your collection on open shelves. Plastic wrap can be used to cover open boxes in which fossils are displayed. As your collection grows, an old bureau, bookcase, or cabinet may be desirable to house the collection.

BRACHIOPODS   *3.*

Collected by: *Peter Nugent*

Date: *June 30, 1969*

Locality: *Roseboom, N. Y.*

Taken from ledge in Mrs. Zimmerman's field.

What Is It?

On the following pages are examples of the different kinds of invertebrate fossils you are most likely to find. The fossils are arranged according to the large group, or phylum, to which they belong. With each group a few living representatives are shown. The scientific names of these fossils can be found on page 51.

MOLLUSKS (CEPHALOPODS)

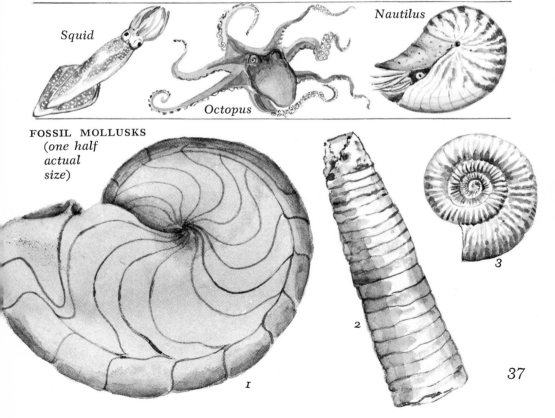

Squid

Octopus

Nautilus

FOSSIL MOLLUSKS
(one half
actual
size)

1

2

3

37

Mollusks (Pelecypods)

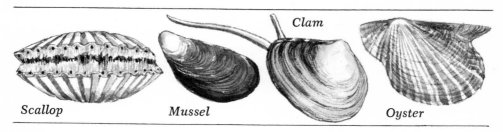

Scallop *Mussel* *Clam* *Oyster*

FOSSIL MOLLUSKS

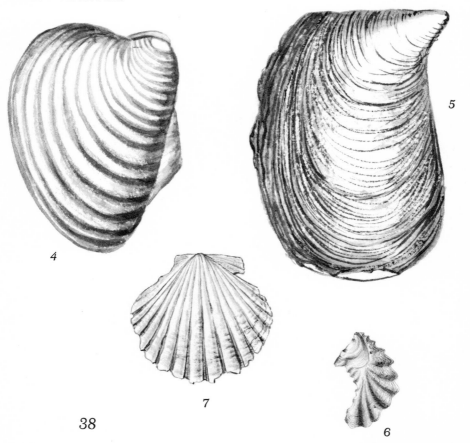

4

5

7

6

38

Mollusks (Gastropods)

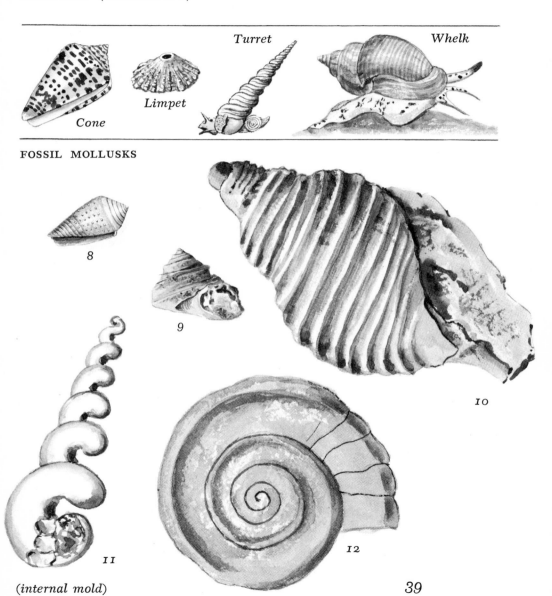

Turret

Whelk

Limpet

Cone

FOSSIL MOLLUSKS

8

9

10

11

(internal mold)

12

Lamp Shells

Lingula

FOSSIL BRACHIOPODS

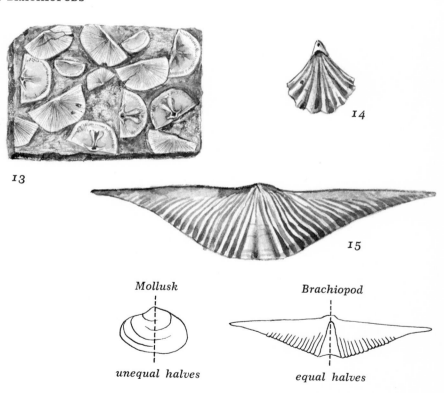

13

14

15

Mollusk

Brachiopod

unequal halves

equal halves

At first glance, brachiopods may be mistaken for mollusks. This diagram shows how to tell these two groups apart.

COELENTERATES

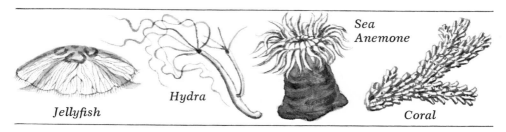

Jellyfish

Hydra

*Sea
Anemone*

Coral

FOSSIL COELENTRATES

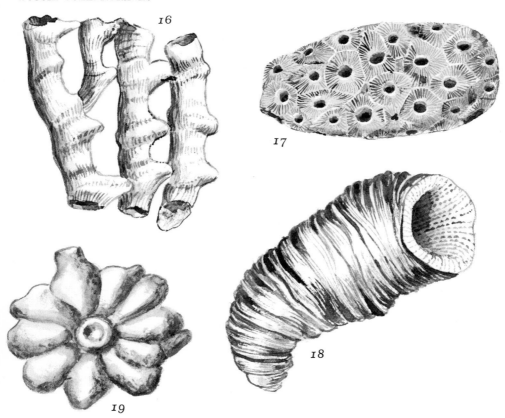

16

17

18

19

41

ECHINODERMS

Starfish

Sea Lily

Brittle
Star

FOSSIL ECHINODERMS

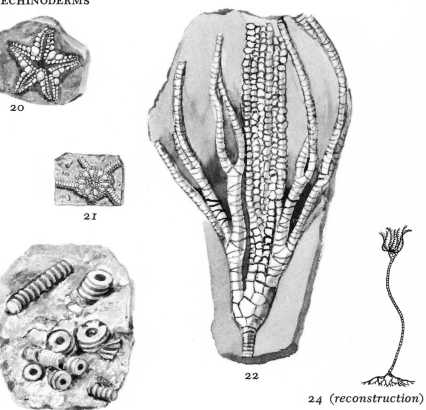

20

21

22

23

24 (reconstruction)

ECHINODERMS

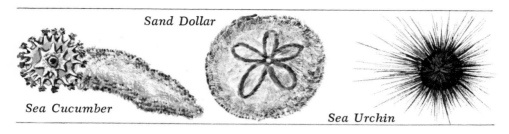

Sea Cucumber   Sand Dollar   Sea Urchin

FOSSIL ECHINODERMS

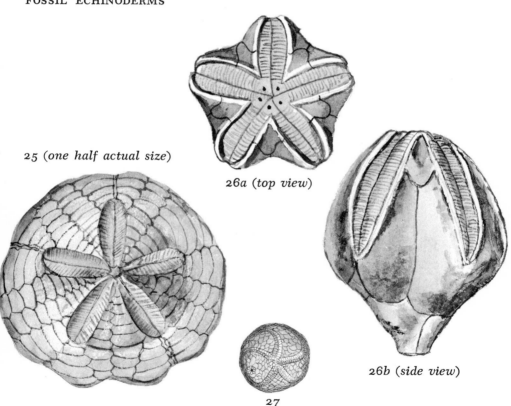

25 (one half actual size)

26a (top view)

26b (side view)

27

BRYOZOANS

Encrusting bryozoan colony

Erect branching bryozoan colony

FOSSIL BRYOZOANS

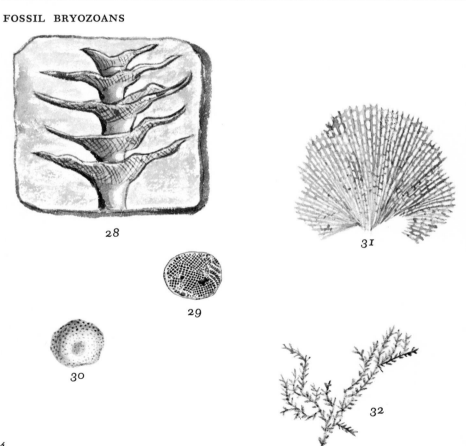

28

29

30

31

32

44

SPONGES

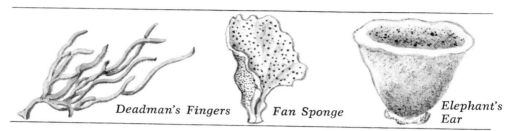

Deadman's Fingers   Fan Sponge   Elephant's Ear

FOSSIL SPONGES

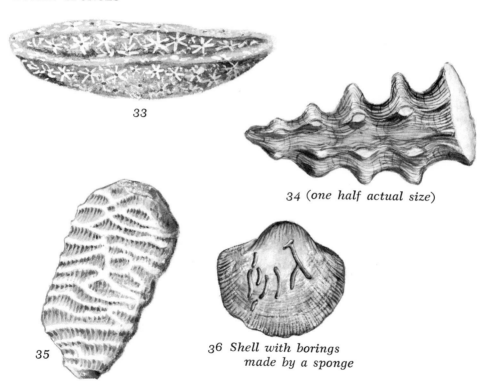

33

34 (one half actual size)

35

36 Shell with borings
made by a sponge

45

ARTHROPODS

Butterfly

Ladybug

Crab

Limulus

FOSSIL ARTHROPODS

37 (one half actual size)

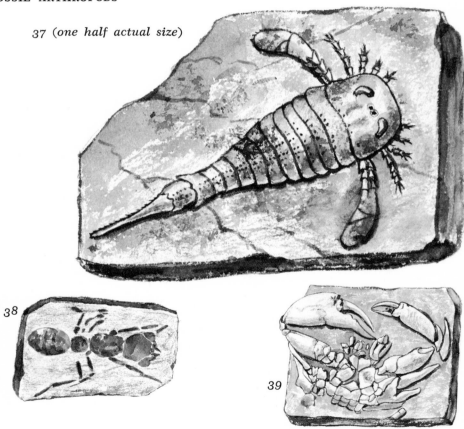

38

39

46

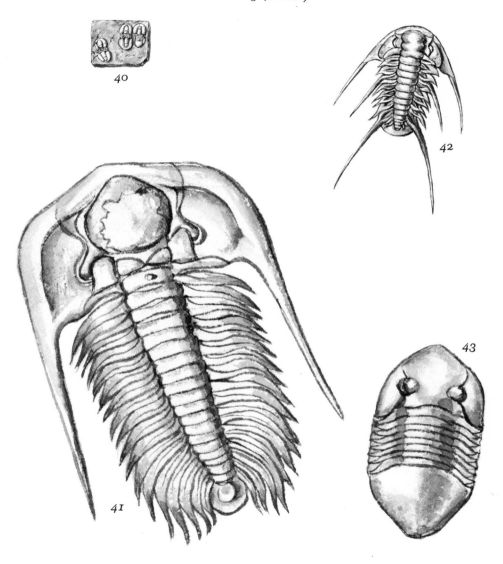

Plant Fossils

In some areas plant fossils may be more common than those of animals. Some of the common types of plant fossils are shown below. The scientific names of these fossils can be found on page 52. Their common names are given below.

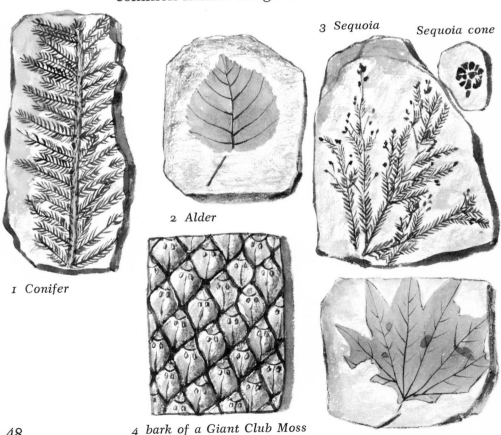

3 Sequoia

Sequoia cone

2 Alder

1 Conifer

4 bark of a Giant Club Moss

5 Sycamore leaf

6 *vinelike plant*

7 *Fern*

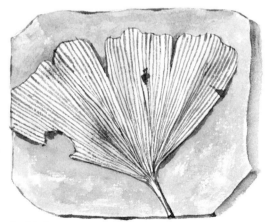

8 *Ginkgo*

9 *Fern*

Petrified Pine Logs at Painted Desert, Arizona

Scientific Names of the Fossils Illustrated

As there are no popular names for these fossils the scientific names are used to identify them.

INVERTEBRATE FOSSILS

MOLLUSKS

CEPHALOPODS
1 Aturia vanuxemi
2 Orthoceras
3 Coeloceras

PELECYPODS
4 Grammysioidea alveata
5 Myalina subquadrata
6 Ostrea mesenterica
7 Chlamys estrellanus

GASTROPODS
8 Conus waltonensis
9 Trochonema umbilicatum
10 Neptunea lirata
11 Turritella
12 Euomphalus latus

BRACHIOPODS
13 Sowerbyella punctostriata
14 Rhynchotreta americana
15 Mucrospirifer mucronatus

COELENTERATES
16 Eridophyllum seriale
17 Hexagonaria percarinata
18 Heliophyllum halli
19 Brooksella alternata

ECHINODERMS
20 Hudsonaster narrawayi
21 Ophiura marylandica
22 Culmicrinus elegans
23 Encrinal limestone with Crinoid stems and discs
24 Complete Crinoid (reconstruction)
25 Scutella aberti
26a & b Pentremites obesus
27 Isorophus cincinnatiensis

BRYOZOANS
28 Archimedes wortheni
29 Rhombotrypa quadrata
30 Ceramopora imbricata
31 Polypora incepta
32 Hederella filiformis

SPONGES
33 Astraeospongium meniscus
34 Hydnoceras bathense
35 Nevadocoelia wistae
36 Clionoides thomasi borings in brachiopod shell

ARTHROPODS
37 Eurypterus remipes
38 *Ant*
39 Zanthopsis vulgaris

Arthropods (*continued*)

TRILOBITES

40 Agnostus montis
41 Paradoxides harlani

42 Albertella helena
43 Isotelus gigas

PLANT FOSSILS

1 Walchia
2 Alnus carpinoides
3 Sequoia affinis
4 Lepidodendron clypeatum

5 Platanus
6 Sphenophyllum
7 Archaeopteris latifolia
8 Ginkgo digitata
9 Phlebopteris smithii

Most of the illustrations in this book were made from specimens, photographs, and published sources. Among the latter the following were especially helpful: *Index Fossils of North America* by Hervey Woodburn Shimer and Robert Rakes Shrock (in particular those figures from publications of the United States Geological Survey, the paleontologic reports of New York and other states, and photographs by Dr. G. Arthur Cooper), *The Fossil Book* by Carroll Lane Fenton and Mildred Adams Fenton, *Invertebrate Paleontology* by William H. Easton, *An Introduction to Paleobotany* by C. A. Arnold, *Plants of the Past* by F. H. Knowlton, *Animals Without Backbones* by Ralph Buchsbaum, and *Fossils* by Frank H. T. Rhodes, Herbert S. Zim, and Paul R. Shaffer.

Bibliography

Animals Without Backbones by Ralph Buchsbaum, The University of Chicago Press, Chicago, Illinois, 1969. 405 pages.
  The standard reference on living invertebrates for college students, it has hundreds of excellent photographs and drawings of this large and varied group of animals.
Discovering Rocks and Minerals by Roy A. Gallant and Christopher J. Schuberth, The Natural History Press, Garden City, New York, 1967. 127 pages.
  This book has chapters on reading topographic and geologic maps, on how rocks are made, on telling geologic time and dating rocks, and a lengthy list of state geological surveys.
The Fossil Book by Carroll Lane Fenton and Mildred Adams Fenton, Doubleday & Company, Inc., New York, 1959. 482 pages.
  Although the text is quite technical, you will be able to learn a great deal about fossils by looking at the many photographs and other excellent illustrations. Try comparing the illustrations with your own fossils. This book will help you to identify your specimens, and to give them their scientific names.
Fossils by Frank H. T. Rhodes, Herbert S. Zim, and Paul R. Shaffer, A Golden Nature Guide, Golden Press, New York, 1962. 160 pages.
  This book, available in paperback, has color illustrations of many invertebrate and plant fossils. It also deals with vertebrates, animals with backbones. Reconstructions of plant and animal life during past periods are included.
Fossils in America by Jay Ellis Ransom, Harper & Row, Publishers, New York, 1964. 402 pages.
Hunting for Fossils by Marian Murray, The Macmillan Company, New York, 1967. 348 pages.
  Both of the above books give detailed information on sites in each state where fossils may be found, the most common fossils in each area, and other helpful information.

Index Fossils of North America by Hervey Woodburn Shimer and Robert Rakes Shrock, The M.I.T. Press, Cambridge, Massachusetts, 1944. 837 pages.

A very technical reference written for the serious student and professional paleontologist. The thousands of illustrations should prove helpful in finding the scientific names of the fossils in your collection.

In Prehistoric Seas by Carroll Lane Fenton and Mildred Adams Fenton, Doubleday & Company, Inc., New York, 1963. 128 pages.

A beautifully illustrated book written for younger readers.

Rockhound Buyers Guide published annually by the *Lapidary Journal*, P.O. Box 2369, San Diego, California 92112.

Every year the April issue of the *Lapidary Journal* lists dealers and gem and mineral clubs throughout the United States and Canada, with information on when and where the clubs meet.

Wonders of Fossils by William H. Matthews III, Dodd, Mead & Company, New York, 1968. 64 pages.

A reference for young readers.

Where to obtain topographic and geologic maps:

West of the Mississippi River and including all of Louisiana and Minnesota:

U.S. Geological Survey
Federal Center
Denver, Colorado 80202

East of the Mississippi River

U.S. Geological Survey
U.S. Department of the Interior
Washington, D.C. 20025

Canada:

Surveys and Mapping Branch
Canada Department of Mines and Technical Surveys
Ottawa, Ontario, Canada

Index

56

Pennsylvanian period, 14, 15, 16
Permian period, 15
petrifaction process, 2–3
plants, 1, 7, 8
  coal and, 12
  common fossil types of, 48–50
Precambrian era, 15
pseudofossils, 10–11

quarries, 21, 26, 28
Quaternary period, 15

record-keeping, *see* data
road maps, 20–21
rock:
  age-dating of, 14–15
  laws protecting, 27
  petrifaction of fossils, 2–3
  pseudofossils in, 10–11
  sedimentary, 9, 12–13, 21, 27–28, 29, 30
  splitting of, 29

safety, 23, 25, 31, 33
sand, 8, 9, 12
sandstone, 12
scouring rush, 16
sea, the, 8–9, 18
sea lily, 18, 42

sedimentary rock, 12–13, 21, 28, 30
  layer formation of, 9, 27, 29
seed fern, 16–17
shale, 12
Silurian period, 15
snail, 6, 8–9, 18
specimens, 30–32
  broken, 32, 34
  cleaning of, 33–34
  display of, 36
  numbering of, 35
sponges, 7, 45
storage, 36

Tertiary period, 15
topographic maps, 21, 54
Triassic period, 15
tuff, 12

United States, 1
  prehistoric, 16–17
  sedimentary rock of, 12, 13
United States Geological Survey, 21, 54

volcanic ash, 8, 12

well diggings, 19, 28
worms, 1, 6, 7
wrapping materials, 24, 31, 36

ABOUT THE AUTHORS

Lois J. Hussey was first attracted to natural history during her childhood in Oyster Bay, Long Island. Her interest grew and she went on to be graduated from Adelphi University with a degree in biology. She was able to develop her interests when she took a position with the Department of Education of the American Museum of Natural History. For more than twenty years she engaged in teaching and administrative work for the Museum. In addition she found time to write. She is co-author, with Catherine Pessino, of *Collecting Cocoons,* a highly successful book for young readers.

In private life, Mrs. Douglas E. Heilbrun, the author now makes her home in Flushing, New York.

Catherine Pessino is a native New Yorker. She was graduated from Hunter College with a degree in biology, and then joined the Department of Education of the American Museum of Natural History. Here she was one of a group of Department members who were instrumental in the establishment of a Natural Science Center for Young People. The Center's exhibits and programs teach New York children about geology, plant and animal life.

Since 1960, Miss Pessino has been head of the Natural Science Center. She has also participated in several exciting research projects for the Museum. She spent two summers in Alaska with the tundra Eskimos. More recently she helped to establish an extensive research program studying two species of tern on Great Gull Island in Long Island Sound.

ABOUT THE ILLUSTRATOR

"Nature was always one of my main interests," writes Anne Marie Jauss, and it is an interest that is reflected in all aspects of her life.

Miss Jauss was born in Munich, Germany, where she studied art at the art school of the state. She left Germany in 1932 to live in Lisbon, Portugal, where she often collected rocks, shells, and some fossils. Her home is now in northern New Jersey.

Illustrator of over sixty books for young people, Anne Marie Jauss has written a number of books as well.